FLUTE

Audio arrangements by Peter Deneff

To access audio visit:
www.halleonard.com/mylibrary
Enter Code
7223-4938-1663-8717

ISBN 978-1-70516-354-2

Visit Hal Leonard Online at
www.halleonard.com

Contact us:
Hal Leonard
7777 West Bluemound Road
Milwaukee, WI 53213
Email: info@halleonard.com

In Europe, contact:
Hal Leonard Europe Limited
42 Wigmore Street
Marylebone, London, W1U 2RN
Email: info@halleonardeurope.com

In Australia, contact:
Hal Leonard Australia Pty. Ltd.
4 Lentara Court
Cheltenham, Victoria, 3192 Australia
Email: info@halleonard.com.au

ALL OF YOU

Flute

Music and Lyrics by
LIN-MANUEL MIRANDA

mp

p

COLOMBIA, MI ENCANTO

FLUTE

Music and Lyrics by
LIN-MANUEL MIRANDA

THE FAMILY MADRIGAL

FLUTE

Music and Lyrics by
LIN-MANUEL MIRANDA

DOS ORUGUITAS

FLUTE

Music and Lyrics by
LIN-MANUEL MIRANDA

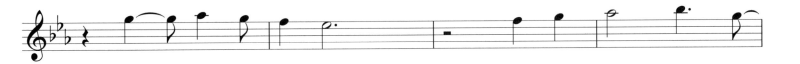

SURFACE PRESSURE

FLUTE

Music and Lyrics by
LIN-MANUEL MIRANDA

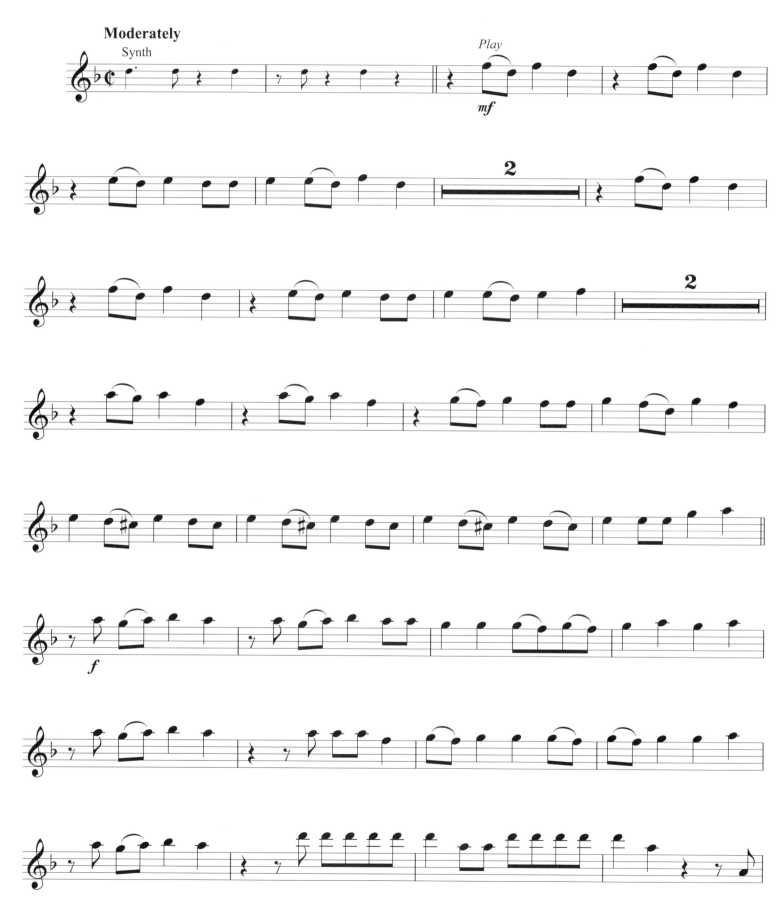

WAITING ON A MIRACLE

Flute

Music and Lyrics by
LIN-MANUEL MIRANDA

rit.

WE DON'T TALK ABOUT BRUNO

FLUTE

Music and Lyrics by
LIN-MANUEL MIRANDA

WHAT ELSE CAN I DO?

Music and Lyrics by
LIN-MANUEL MIRANDA

FLUTE